Today is

1

"My throat is so sore," says Neil. "It BURNS. I'd better stay in bed all day."

2

"You'll miss your test!" says his dad.

Neil makes a sad face.

"You'll miss your friend's party, too!" his mom says.

Neil had forgotten about the party!

"Maybe I'll feel okay this afternoon," Neil says.

"No, you'd better stay in bed ALL day," Neil's parents tell him.